W9-BGZ-004

COUGARS

EYE TO EYE WITH BIG CATS

Jason Cooper

Rourke

Publishing LLC

Vero Beach, Florida 32964

www.rourkepublishing.com

PHOTO CREDITS: All photos © Lynn M. Stone

Cover Photo: *Cougars are found from the mountains of Canada to the jungles of South America.*

Editor: Frank Sloan

Cover design by Nicola Stratford

Library of Congress Cataloging-in-Publication Data

Cooper, Jason, 1942-
  Cougars / Jason Cooper.
    p. cm. — (Eye to eye with big cats)
Summary: Describes the physical characteristics, habitat, and life cycle of cougars.
Includes bibliographical references and index.
  ISBN 1-58952-402-0 (hardcover)
  1. Puma—Juvenile literature. [1. Puma.] I. Title.

QL737.C23 C6745 2002
599.75'24--dc21

                                            2002003651

Printed in the USA

CG/CG

TABLE OF CONTENTS

THE COUGAR

The cougar is a **mammal** that lives in many parts of North and South America. In fact, the cougar *(Felis concolor)* has the biggest **range** of any American mammal.

The cougar is also known by many other names. Mountain lion, puma, panther, catamount, and painter are all names for the same creature.

THE COUGAR'S RELATIVES

The cougar is a **feline**, a member of the cat family. Other large cats include jaguars, leopards, tigers, and lions.

The cougar has the typical fangs, claws, short jaws, and graceful movements of all cats. The cougar, however, is not like some of the other big cats. For example, the cougar cannot roar. The other large cats can. But a cougar purrs like a house cat.

A Florida panther perches on an oak limb.

WHAT COUGARS LOOK LIKE

Cougars have small heads and long necks attached to big, low-slung bodies. The fur is usually brown or gray with white underneath. Cougars have long, thick tails. These tails may help them climb and jump.

Male cougars weigh about 160 pounds (72.5 kilograms). Females weigh 90 to 135 pounds (41 to 61 kilograms). The largest known cougar weighed 276 pounds (125 kilograms).

A cougar in the Rocky Mountains races after a rabbit.

WHERE COUGARS LIVE

Cougars live from northern Canada, through the United States, Central America, and into Argentina. They live mostly in western Canada and in the western United States. There are a few cougars in the eastern United States.

The cougar's home, or **habitat**, can be forest, brush land, grassland, or **semi desert**. Cougars in Florida live at sea level. They have also been found in the South American mountains as high as 14,800 feet (4,511 meters).

A cougar follows the valley of the Flathead River in Montana.

A cougar steps quietly through a jungle in Central America.

A mountain lion, one of the many names for a cougar

HOW COUGARS LIVE

Cougars usually hunt at night. This means they are called **nocturnal** animals. If prey is scarce, however, then they may have to hunt in daylight. Cougars have fine hearing and eyesight as well as a good sense of smell.

Like most cats, cougars have home **territories**. A cougar marks the edges of its territory with urine and claw marks on trees.

Cougars are at home in deep snow.

COUGAR CUBS

A mother cougar usually has three or four spotted kittens, or cubs. Cubs are born blind in a cave or another hiding place. Their eyes open in about two weeks.

At about six weeks, the cubs may be taken by the mother on a kill. The spots disappear during the end of the kittens' first year. By the age of 20 to 22 months, the cubs have learned to **stalk.** They kill their prey. At this time, the cubs leave the mother.

A mother cougar licks her kitten.

PREDATOR AND PREY

Cougars are **predators**, or hunters. They will eat almost any animal they can catch, but deer are a favorite **prey**. A cougar hides its kills and returns to them for several meals.

Cougars stalk prey by moving very slowly toward an animal and crouching. When the cougar is close to its prey, it leaps out of hiding and pounces. A cougar has teeth and the strength to kill an animal up to seven times its size.

A cougar dines on deer, a favorite prey.

COUGARS AND PEOPLE

The native people of the Americas have generally respected cougars. The Cherokee Indians said the cougar was the greatest of wild hunters. Cougars rarely kill farm animals and are almost never a threat to people.

Cougars are now completely protected by law in many states. In others, they are "big game" animals. This means they can be hunted only during certain seasons.

Although it is the state mammal, the Florida panther is nearly extinct.

THE FUTURE OF COUGARS

Many people in cougar country are glad to know that cougars are in the wilderness. However, when the wilderness disappears, so do the cougars. However, if humans protect the cougar, their numbers could increase.

No one knows whether the cougar will make a comeback in the East. The panther is the state mammal in Florida. However, there may only be as few as 30 to 50 panthers left in the state. The animal is in danger of becoming **extinct**.

GLOSSARY

extinct (eks TINKT) — no longer existing

feline (FEE line) — of the cat family

habitat (HAB uh tat) — the area in which an animal lives

mammal (MAM uhl) — a group of animals that produce milk and have either fur or hair

nocturnal (nock TERN uhl) — active at night

predators (PRED uh turz) — animals that kill other animals for food

prey (PRAY) — an animal that is hunted for food by another animal

range (RAYNJ) — an area where animals may roam and feed

semi desert (SEM ee DEZ urt) — an area like a true desert but not as dry

stalk (STAWK) — to hunt by slowly and quietly moving toward prey

territories (TARE uh TOR eez) — home areas defended by certain animals that live within it

INDEX

Further Reading

Corrigan, Patricia. *Cougars*. NorthWord Press, 2001

St. Pierre, Stephanie. *Cougars*. Heinemann Library, 2001

Websites To Visit

http://www.panther.state.fl.us/

http://www.dfg.ca.gov/lion

http://puma.home.texas.net/pumadescription.html

About The Author

Jason Cooper has written several children's books about a variety of topics for Rourke Publishing, including recent series *China Discovery* and *American Landmarks*. Cooper travels widely to gather information for his books. Two of his favorite travel destinations are Alaska and the Far East.